BOLD

BO

212 Charisma and Small Talk Tips to
Engage, Charm and Leave a Lasting Impression

TYCHO
PRESS

Contents

Introduction

Being charismatic has forever been the holy grail of personality skills. The ability to charm and delight others, to playfully switch between the serious and the trivial, to make others feel important, interesting, indispensable; the talent of shining a light on someone and letting them immerse in its warmth, the genius of transcending cultural, language, age and other barriers and becoming instantly relevant and absorbing, as well as a myriad other skills—all these combined are what charismatic people do.

You will be told by other authors and all sorts of image and PR gurus, who are as transient as a fabric trend in a fashion season, that you can feign charisma. That, if only you mimicked that person, or acquired that habit, or said that thing (and so on to exhaustion), you will immediately start enjoying the same responses and social success of famous people, keynote speakers, gifted leaders. The truth is otherwise, however.

Charisma is a gift, the same way writing music like Mozart is a gift. Anyone can learn to play an instrument, even become extremely skilled and eventually a virtuoso. But composing like Mozart did, no amount of schooling can get you there. Similarly, you can take all the classes, read all the books, and watch all the videotapes on how to develop a charismatic personality and become an expert conversationalist. You can devour the entire "pickup artist" literature and attend leadership seminars. Even if you devote all your free time to becoming a charismatic person, the divide between an extremely skilled person (the piano virtuoso) and the charismatic person (Mozart) will always be there.

There is, however, one way to game the system. Although charisma requires much more than any single book can directly teach you, it is also not an entirely "genetic" trait. Schooling, manners, etiquette and, most of all, practice will build your demeanor, improve your conversation techniques, expand your circle of friends and acquaintances, increase your invitations to events, introduce you to new people and social settings. And, who knows, you might have actually had a charismatic person hidden inside you all along who never had the chance to come out.

This is the purpose of this book, then: I will tell you (and show you) all the things you need to be aware of in your interactions. Some advice will come in the form of explicit tips, or warnings. Some of it will come humorously through the use of cartoons and jokes. More yet will be in the form of quotes from famous people embodying the spirit that makes up a charismatic personality. By working on the level of the conscious teaching, of the subconscious witticism, the visual as well as the textual, the obvious and the subtle, this book will turn you into a social genius, a master of the conversation and an expert in attracting other people's praise.

From Hermit to Sociable

PART ONE

n case your social life has taken a hit since high school, either because of studies or work, it's time to rekindle your interest in other people and their life stories. It's also important to develop the basic skills necessary to navigate a work lunch, an invitation to a casual dinner, or the opening night of a friend's exhibition. This first part will walk you through life's least demanding social happenings and provide you with essential etiquette rules for making a proper (and pleasantly memorable, but not intimidating) appearance.

"Manners are
the ability to put
someone at their
ease . . . by turning
any answer
into another
question."

—TINA BROWN

Use people's names.

People nowadays have no reservations about standing right next to someone and referring to them with a pronoun, ("him," "her," "he," or "she"). Nothing can be more off-putting, never mind rude. Make a point of saying people's names when you are speaking about them in their company; they will appreciate it, and so will others who are present. Also, refrain from reducing them to the role they play in your life. Designators such as "my wife" or "my boss" may get a pass the first time you mention them, just to make everyone aware of the relationship. After that, use their names.

Look your conversation partner in the eyes.

Address partners, spouses, assistants, friends.

When you are interested in charming someone, make sure you also acknowledge their partners, their spouses, their friends, their assistants, etc. Focusing just on the person you're interested in might flatter them, but will most likely annoy and frustrate everyone else. That's where flattery can backfire. Give everyone your equal and undivided attention.

Use empathizers.

Every now and then, try to sprinkle conversation with empathizers such as, "I see what you mean," "I completely agree with you," or "That's a lovely thing to say." Even if you proceed to take a different viewpoint, having commending others for the way they think, and the way they're expressing themselves, is a heartwarming gesture. Make sure you don't overdo it, lest you get labeled a blatant flatterer. But a short expression of empathy with the other person will make your consent all the more believable, and your differences (if there are any) much more agreeable.

16

Don't look at your cell phone during any interaction.

PERSONAL | SOCIAL | BUSINESS

Stand tall—yes, physically.

Advisors and image makers always have a lot to say about posture and presence. That's because visual impact is immediate and long-lasting. Our bodies are canvases on which emotions, temperaments, experiences, and attitudes become physically manifest. Whether consciously or deliberately, we use body language and posture to send messages. Standing tall is a metaphor that communicates elegance, sincerity, dependability, confidence, and composure. It should be one of the most self-evident parts of your public image. Always be aware of your posture and carry yourself—metaphorically and physically—with grace and self-assurance. The effect on others will be immediately apparent.

HERMIT ⟶ SOCIABLE

Always hold the door open for other people.

Give your undivided attention, body language included.

When you are addressing someone, or someone is addressing you, make sure to signal that you are completely engaged. That means maintaining eye contact (even when there are distractions), nodding in agreement, remaining emotionally responsive, facing the person you are speaking with, and presenting a general appearance of openness. All those elements will signal that you are physically present and, more importantly, that you are mentally and emotionally receptive. Being this way will also encourage your partner to offer more.

HERMIT ⟶ SOCIABLE

"Darling, please say you'll marry me . . ."

Keep hand gestures away from your face.

Gesturing is an art, and it doesn't translate easily across cultures. Some people tend to be more physically expressive than others. They use gestures for even the most pedestrian of conversations. Like the volume of your voice, "loud" gestures irritate, and even intimidate, physically subtle people. This is especially true of gestures around your face. When your hands touch your face, it can signal that you're nervous or lying (as when you place them in front of your mouth or brush the tip of your eyebrow), frustrated (as when you clasp your head), or vexed (pinching your nostrils). Remember the famous sculpture by Rodin, *The Thinker*? The Thinker's chin rests on his fist—indicative of contemplation, solitude, and introspection. In social settings, avoid even this calm gesture. Signal to your companions that you are engaged in a straightforward manner.

HERMIT ⟶ SOCIABLE

"You have to learn the rules of the game. And then you have to play better than anyone else."

—ALBERT EINSTEIN

Don't yawn when someone is talking.

Dress for the occasion.

No detail goes unnoticed. For better or worse, that extends to your clothes. Knowing what to wear doesn't mean overdressing. Dressing up can be just as off-putting as dressing down—although it's admittedly safer. But going with the safer choice isn't the same as going with the right choice; it still suggests you don't know how to dress. Wearing the right clothes for an occasion shows that you understand the nature of the event. If you're not sure what to wear, spend a little time researching the occasion you'll be attending. It shows respect for your host, potential employer, future business partner, or future life partner. It indicates that you are a versatile, tasteful, and thoughtful guest.

HERMIT $\longrightarrow$ SOCIABLE

Match the occasion
to the dress code

1	Dinner party at someone's home	A	Pin-striped suit
2	Job interview	B	Tuxedo
3	Romantic date	C	Casual suit
4	Meeting with a realtor	D	Tracksuit
5	Wedding party at the Plaza Hotel	E	Blazer and jeans
6	Hiking	F	Casual shirt and khakis

Correct answer: 1-E, 2-A, 3-C, 4-F, 5-B, 6-D

HERMIT ⟶ SOCIABLE

"No act of kindness, however small, is ever lost."

—AESOP

Respect the private areas in your host's home.

Do at least one good deed a day.

Doing good makes us feel good about ourselves. Your good deed can be extremely small, and it doesn't have to be public. (In fact, a private gesture is better.) You may not be able to change the world, but you can change one person's life, even if just for an instant. Any good deed, regardless of scale, matters. You'll feel good about yourself, and that will magnify your self-confidence.

HERMIT ⟶ SOCIABLE

Don't get drunk at social events.

Ask questions that show you're interested.

Showing interest in what another person has to say makes them feel compelling, and important. The best way to demonstrate that interest is to ask for more. Asking your conversation partners questions about what they have said sends a message that you are not just a passive listener; you are an engaged and attentive person who is interested in their story, idea, or plan. Asking questions that are relevant and specific is central to having a great conversation. But make sure your questions move the conversation forward, rather than express doubt or interrogate. Displaying suspicion and skepticism is alienating and divisive; being genuinely curious is a sign of charisma.

PERSONAL

SOCIAL

BUSINESS

"People don't care
how much you
know until they
know how much
you care."

—JOHN MAXWELL

Be courteous, even if it seems old-fashioned.

PERSONAL

SOCIAL

BUSINESS

Focus first on the delivery, then the words.

If delivery was irrelevant, then anyone could be a great actor. This is not to say that you must act everything that comes out of your mouth. But the tone of your voice, your body posture, the look in your eyes, and your general demeanor should be fine-tuned to match the mood and content of your words. An impassioned speech can be much more impactful than a bland and wooden delivery, even if the words are identical. Delivery doesn't make your point different, but it will make sure that your point is more effective and clear. Of course, *what* you say matters. Good content, coupled with great delivery, is an unbeatable combination. Don't stumble, don't question yourself at the moment you speak—come across as confident and give the impression that you own your opinion.

HERMIT ⟶ SOCIABLE

"Anyone who ever gave you confidence, you owe them a lot."

—TRUMAN CAPOTE

PERSONAL

SOCIAL

BUSINESS

Don't leave a mess in your host's bathroom.

Have a variety of positive reactions, not the same generic smile for everyone.

If you gave every person you knew flowers on Valentine's Day, it would raise an eyebrow, to say the least. Some gestures are meant to make others feel special. When they're offered indiscriminately, they lose their meaning and, ultimately, their value. In the same way, when addressing others, be sure to vary your approach, your expressions, your reactions, your words. Don't do so in an overdramatic fashion; people might think you're deranged or just awkward. Introduce subtle differences, individualized "treats" that will make others feel special.

HERMIT ⎯⎯⎯→ SOCIABLE

"You sure know how to fill an awkward lull in the conversation."

Be mindful of your jokes.

Being funny is a great icebreaker. Everyone lists humor as a personality trait they look for in a leader, friend, partner, or social acquaintance. But jokes have a way of telling the truth, even when we don't intend them to. It's important, when you are telling jokes—especially in the company of people you don't know well—to observe cultural boundaries. Be wary of offending, expressing negative thoughts and opinions, and crossing the line into the unsavory. Excusing yourself with the justification that "it was just a joke" won't cut it. (If you say that, you have certainly committed a faux pas.) People are not always as oblivious as we'd like them to be; they can read between the lines more acutely than we sometimes think.

SOCIAL

Remember...

If your hosts are older than you	
If your hosts are professionally senior to you	**DON'T SWEAR**
If your hosts are old-fashioned	
If your hosts are Mormon	
If your hosts don't like foul language	
If there are children around	
If you are eager to make a good impression	

Try to avoid un-PC topics and jokes.

Remember the little details.

Bits of information that people give you may seem trivial, but they carry a great deal of significance for them. Names, places, education, career moves, their hometown, the niece's birthday party they attended last week, their favorite book, a movie they recently watched that made a lasting impression—all these seem like unimportant details, but they make up a huge part of people's lives. When you show that you remember them, it communicates that you pay attention and really care. That's especially true if the other person is not so good at remembering these small details; they are bound to be impressed by your ability to retain information and ask about it in subsequent conversations.

PERSONAL

HERMIT ⟶ SOCIABLE

"Do you have a 'Belated Happy Wedding Anniversary' card?"

Do your homework.

If the event you're attending—regardless of how big or small, whether professional or social—has a dominant theme, do some research on the subject beforehand. Before going to a movie party, read about the film. It pays to be well-informed about the topic people will be talking about. You will fit in more naturally, you'll have more to say, your company will be more coveted, and you will be less bored yourself.

44

HERMIT ⟶ SOCIABLE

Always RSVP, even if it is to decline an invitation.

Don't show up at a party (dinner or otherwise) empty-handed.

Don't discuss unpleasant topics over dinner; it's the time to break bread.

There is an old saying: If silence falls over the dinner table, either the food is good or the company is bad. The dinner table is not the place to discuss controversial or unpleasant topics. The dinner table is a place, literally and metaphorically, to break bread, enjoy each other's company, discuss "safe" topics, and make pleasant conversation. Anyone who brings up delicate issues or, even worse, encourages confrontation is likely to upset others—both their moods and their stomachs.

HERMIT $\longrightarrow$ SOCIABLE

Don't leave the television on when people visit.

"'Stay' is a charming word in a friend's vocabulary."

—LOUISA MAY ALCOTT

PERSONAL

SOCIAL

BUSINESS

When someone tells you what they do for living, respond, "Wow, that's impressive."

For most people, work is a means to an end. Whether they love what they do or not, they spend a considerable amount of their life doing it. Giving someone credit for their hard work is extremely flattering. Even if a person's profession seems easy and pleasant, you can boost their sense of accomplishment by assuming, and expressing, that it is still hard. You will imply they possess talents and character traits you admire. It will invariably make them open up and they will leave the discussion feeling appreciated.

HERMIT ⟶ SOCIABLE

Greet your guests when they arrive.

PERSONAL

SOCIAL

BUSINESS

Social Heat

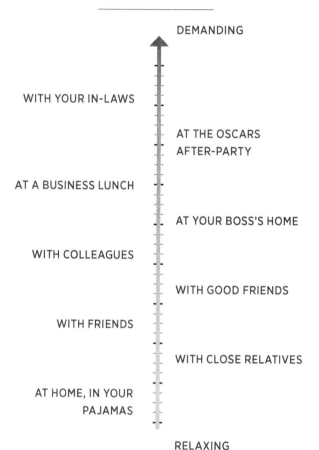

DEMANDING

WITH YOUR IN-LAWS

AT THE OSCARS
AFTER-PARTY

AT A BUSINESS LUNCH

AT YOUR BOSS'S HOME

WITH COLLEAGUES

WITH GOOD FRIENDS

WITH FRIENDS

WITH CLOSE RELATIVES

AT HOME, IN YOUR
PAJAMAS

RELAXING

HERMIT ⟶ SOCIABLE

SOCIAL

Be emotionally expressive.

Displaying emotion can be perceived as a sign of weakness. But being emotionally responsive is one of the best ways to get others to open up. Without exaggerating your reactions, show that you are in touch with your feelings. This makes you look more human, which translates to "compassionate" and "approachable." People who are emotionally expressive are more likely to win the attention and sympathy of others, and are far more successful at making spontaneous connections with strangers.

HERMIT ⟶ SOCIABLE

Be punctual, especially for seated dinners.

Even when you know where the conversation is going, don't interrupt.

This is elementary. Being interrupted while speaking is extremely annoying. Talking isn't just the expression of a fully formed thought; sometimes talking is part of the thinking process. In other words, we are sometimes forming a sentence or processing an idea as we are expressing it. Speaking seems natural, but to express a coherent thought takes effort; some people have more trouble than others. Interrupting others isn't just bad manners; it sabotages your partner's ability to think and speak. Even if you know where the discussion is going—even if you've heard it all before, even if you are becoming anxious or impatient—never, *never* interrupt another person in the middle of their thought.

"Throw away those books and cassettes on inspirational leadership. Send those consultants packing. Know your job, set a good example for the people under you, and put results over politics. That's all the charisma you'll really need to succeed."

—DYAN MACHAN

Ask "What about you?" after you've answered a question.

Humans crave reciprocity. Whether it's love or gifts, giving back is polite, gratifying, and pleasing. When you're asked a question, regardless of whether the topic is mundane or deep, extend the same interest to your conversational counterpart. It will not go unnoticed. Many questions are asked with the sole intent of being asked back. (When someone asks how your weekend was, often they're hoping to talk about theirs). A balanced environment for exchange can only be positive. Keep the giving in line with the receiving.

HERMIT $\longrightarrow$ SOCIABLE

Don't
bring along uninvited guests.

Remember to call or write the next day and thank the host.

Read the news before any social engagement.

Before any social engagement where there's likely to be conversation, find out what's going on in current affairs, politics, art, and popular culture. Paint yourself as a person with a wide variety of interests; show you are engaged in many areas. This insures that, whichever way the conversation veers, you'll have something to say. And, if you get stuck in a slow conversation, drawing attention to today's most newsworthy item can get you gracefully out of the spotlight. Before you head out, turn on the television or read the paper online to get the latest news. Make a few mental notes and off you go.

HERMIT $\longrightarrow$ SOCIABLE

Don't ask if it's okay to smoke unless your host has already lit up (and even then, you still need to ask).

PERSONAL | SOCIAL | BUSINESS

"*I don't* do *lunch, young man,
I* eat *lunch!*"

Expand your vocabulary.

The art of conversation hinges on the beauty of language. Part of telling a tale well is knowing and using the right words. A good vocabulary also makes the speaker more sophisticated; it intrigues most and intimidates opponents. Of course, simply opening the dictionary and inserting big words into your conversation won't work: that'll make you seem pretentious and silly, rather than charismatic. Instead, read long, well-written articles (articles that are more than just informational and news-focused), become engrossed in documentaries (about any topic), or simply watch *Masterpiece Theatre* on PBS.

63

HERMIT ⎯⎯⎯⎯⟶ SOCIABLE

Respect the private space of others at work, even if it's just a countertop or a cubby.

Practice positive reinforcement.

"Positive reinforcement" is a psychology term for rewarding others when they do something you want them to repeat. Punishment shapes behavior by penalizing a wrong choice or action; positive reinforcement works by rewarding right ones. Most studies agree that positive reinforcement is not only more effective than punishment in the short run, it actually creates long-term behavioral patterns and changes a person's perspective. In your relationships, make sure you acknowledge the correct, virtuous, and productive elements, rather than punishing the ones that bother you. The results will be better, and everyone will feel happier.

SOCIAL

BUSINESS

65

Your clothes should always be clean and properly pressed.

Don't eat all the food on any plate except your own; show some restraint.

PERSONAL | SOCIAL | BUSINESS

Don't discuss others' failings and shortcomings.

Unless you are expressly interested in diminishing and belittling another person, there is no reason to publicly advertise their shortcomings. Constructive criticism and objective judgment should be used when the time is right. But demeaning another person in public is useless, especially as a means to make yourself look good. This technique inevitably backfires; it makes you look mean, miserly, and completely insensitive. You will come across as someone who cannot be trusted, who will use any opportunity to promote yourself, even at the cost of embarrassing and hurting others—the least charismatic thing you can do!

HERMIT ⟶ SOCIABLE

Be aware of your body language.

Don't point out speech mistakes.

People make mistakes. Tempting as it may be to feed your ego by pointing out grammatical mistakes, don't. It's ridiculous and pointless. It aggravates everyone, creates unnecessary interruptions, and subconsciously discredits the person speaking. Helping someone who is at a loss for a word is perfectly acceptable, even commendable. But that's very different from interrupting another's train of thought to point out the correct use or pronunciation of a word.

If you make bodily noises, such as a burp, simply say, "Excuse me" and move on.

PERSONAL

SOCIAL

BUSINESS

Delete fillers
(like, you know, sort of…)

A filler is something crammed into open spaces to seal them. The more gaps in your speech, the harder it is to follow. In order to prevent yourself, and others, from falling into the gaps, you plug them with fillers. You may be covering the hole, but everyone still knows it's there. It takes practice and determination, but you need to delete the fillers from your speech. They make you look unsophisticated and slow.

HERMIT ⟶ SOCIABLE

Don't
ask taboo questions: salary, age, marital status.

PERSONAL | SOCIAL | BUSINESS

*"Can you believe that his office refers
to him as a 'superachiever'?"*

"I'm competitive with myself.
I always try to push past my own borders."

—TYRA BANKS

PERSONAL

SOCIAL

BUSINESS

Sin is alleviated through penitence. Crime is followed by punishment. Bad social skills find their justice, too.

SIN	PENANCE
Didn't greet the host	No socializing for a week
Texting during talking	Watch one hour of late-night infomercials
Got drunk and punched guest	Police custody
Stole silver	Return (polish first)
Ate last canapé	30 minutes on the treadmill

HERMIT ----------> SOCIABLE

Don't touch other people, unless they invite you to.

PERSONAL | SOCIAL | BUSINESS

Don't stare (regardless how weird the outfit).

"If you want to conquer fear, don't sit at home and think about it. Go out and get busy."

—DALE CARNEGIE

Not all your thoughts need to be expressed.

Learn to edit what you say. That means paying close attention to the content your mind produces before it ends up on your tongue. You need to shape your thoughts, improve them, and only then should you express yourself. This invariably means that most of your thoughts will remain yours alone, forever hidden from everyone else. The trick is to make this process deliberate. Develop an acute sense of what is appropriate, useful, interesting, constructive, inspiring, and worthwhile. Share that with others and keep the rest to yourself. You will acquire the reputation of a person who speaks less, but says more.

HERMIT ⟶ SOCIABLE

Don't ask what's to eat before accepting a dinner invitation.

PERSONAL | SOCIAL | BUSINESS

From Sociable to Popular

PART TWO

As your social life begins to expand beyond the familiar and intimate and into the deeper waters of social prowess, you must be getting used to the idea that socializing can be an extremely delicate, and exhausting, experience. People may be social creatures, but that doesn't make everyone automatically sociable. You will face challenges, irritable and irritating people, difficult conversation topics, and awkward silences. This section will prove invaluable in conquering them.

PERSONAL

SOCIAL

BUSINESS

"People will forget what you said, people will forget what you did, but people will never forget how you made them feel."

—MAYA ANGELOU

Don't give away your smiles.

Smiling is one of the core human communication tools. It is universal; across cultures and nationalities, everyone smiles. Like everything good, though, its value decreases if it's overused. If you smile all the time, at everyone, on any occasion, it will stop being something special and will, gradually, become your default facial expression. Find a middle ground, where you are neither stiff and reserved nor overly excitable and affectionate. This builds your reputation as someone who is generous and also sincere. Timing is everything.

PERSONAL | SOCIAL | BUSINESS

Don't over-compliment.

Prompt a story with,
"Tell us about that time when ..."

One of the most effective ways to win the admiration of others is to be a friend's conversational wingman. Prompt your friend to tell a story with an opener such as, "Remember when ..." or, "Tell the story with ..." This is a priceless piece of camaraderie and support. Being a wingman makes your friend look great, and makes you look even greater because it accentuates your generosity. And, rest assured, the favor will be returned.

SOCIAL

Be warm.

You are being introduced to someone in the middle of a meal . . .

WRONG	RIGHT
With your mouth still full, take a big gulp of wine to wash the food down. At the same time, tilt your head carelessly back, slightly turn toward them, and mumble, "Hey, I'm _____ (your name)." Continue with your food.	Put your silverware down, wipe your mouth, rest the napkin on the table, and get up. Then give them your hand and say, "Nice to meet you."

SOCIABLE ────────→ POPULAR

Turn the conversation toward your partner, not yourself.

People sometimes tell stories as an indirect way of saying something about themselves. Listening to these tales can sometimes be tiresome. But do it anyway. Be forgiving of the fact that others might want to focus on themselves. You should practice selflessness and turn the conversation toward the other person. Avoid the temptation to refer to yourself and, instead, ask about your partner. Be eager to hear *their* story, *their* stance, how the topic at hand relates to and concerns *them*. Few things will make them feel more important.

SOCIABLE ⟶ POPULAR

Don't point your finger at others.

PERSONAL | SOCIAL | BUSINESS

Pick keywords from what your partner says and build on them.

People prefer acceptance to rejection. The way to say, "I accept you," without saying the words, is to echo another's concerns. Listen carefully for words your partner uses repeatedly; then use them yourself when your turn comes. This takes some practice, and an open ear, but if done properly it can never go wrong. The other person will be pleased they found a conversation partner who shares their vocabulary. If they suspect that you are deliberately using their words, they will be flattered and will admire both your willingness to listen closely and your ability to improvise.

SOCIABLE $\longrightarrow$ POPULAR

Don't push a conversation to its limits.

PERSONAL

SOCIAL

BUSINESS

Make a bold statement, and substantiate it.

There is an excellent way to make a lasting good impression: Make a bold, even audacious (but true) statement that will draw everyone's attention to you. When everyone is hooked, deliver the rest of the story. But be careful; you must deliver. If you don't, you'll look like a brazen sensationalist—and that's the kind way of putting it. Also, make sure your statement is engaging and bold enough, but not insulting or deliberately abrasive, provocative, or contentious. There are good ways and bad ways to get others' attention and arouse their curiosity. Be sure to choose a good one!

STEIN

"Okay, you're a visionary. I'm a visionary. Everybody here is a visionary. But what do you do for a living?"

"A man who wants to lead the orchestra must turn his back on the crowd."

—MAX LUCADO

Embroider "thanks" with a bit more.

Thanking another person for their contribution, support, help, or service is a given. Enrich a dry and short "thanks" with some informal particulars of what you liked, or in what way their action was valuable. You can magnify your expression of gratitude and turn a cliché into sincere appreciation.

SOCIABLE ⟶ POPULAR

PERSONAL

SOCIAL

BUSINESS

Be compassionate.

Always look for opportunities to improve yourself.

The world is always changing. Our personalities, talents, and skills should keep changing too, and adapting to new circumstances. Our brain is a very sophisticated feedback machine. Charismatic people are always on the lookout for ways to improve their personality, expand their skills, and become better at whatever they do. Self-improvement is worthy and rewarding in itself. Whether it comes naturally—through repeated successes and failures—or consciously by reading books, taking on projects, and embracing learning experiences, the idea is to get better and be better.

SOCIABLE ⟶ POPULAR

PERSONAL | SOCIAL | BUSINESS

Don't lose focus and let your mind wander.

"A good leader takes a little more than his share of the blame, a little less than his share of the credit."

—ARNOLD H. GLASGOW

PERSONAL   SOCIAL   BUSINESS

Eat before you go to a party.

Going to a party on an empty stomach is a bad idea. Not only will you be gorging on all the food, which is terribly unattractive, you also will lose valuable networking time staying in the buffet line, filling up your plate, looking for a place to put your empty plate, and so on. You will reduce your active participation by at least 30 to 50 percent just by getting your food and eating it. Although it's not advisable to eat just before going to a dinner or lunch invitation (not touching your food will suggest dissatisfaction), going to a cocktail party or similar function with a full stomach means you maximize what you are there to do in the first place: network.

Party drinking behavioral flowchart

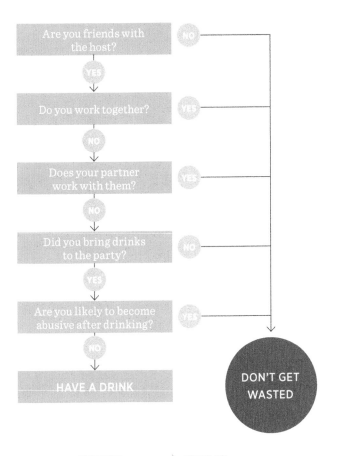

Are you friends with the host?
NO

YES

Do you work together?
YES

NO

Does your partner work with them?
YES

NO

Did you bring drinks to the party?
NO

YES

Are you likely to become abusive after drinking?
YES

NO

HAVE A DRINK

DON'T GET WASTED

SOCIABLE ⟶ POPULAR

Don't talk to anyone for longer than 10 minutes at the beginning of a party.

Make others feel like the most important people in the room.

This is one of the oldest adages of charisma, leadership, and magnetism. And for a reason: it works. Ask questions, make compliments, be engrossed in what you are hearing, let yourself be impressed and affected—in short, behave in ways that will make your conversation partner feel like the most important person in the room, the center of your universe, even if for just a little while. Nothing brings out your own charm like shining the spotlight on another person in a way that makes them feel significant. Remember that light is always reflected.

SOCIABLE $\longrightarrow$ POPULAR

"Does anyone here have enough sense of
security to oppose my suggestion?"

"People buy into the leader before they buy into the vision."

—JOHN C. MAXWELL

PERSONAL

SOCIAL

BUSINESS

Echo the language of others.

The words we use reveal our thoughts, moods, and beliefs.
When you are about to address another person, or a group
of people, listen to how they speak. Are they restrained,
do they avoid swearing, are they loud-mouthed and informal? Being different may intrigue them, but it might also
send a message of rejection or condescension. Try to
match your audience's style; make them feel comfortable.
If you are unfamiliar with specific words and jargon, try
to match the general tone of the majority of the people
you're addressing—or at least of the person you are trying to impress.

Listen more than you talk.

PERSONAL

SOCIAL

BUSINESS

"The most basic of
all human needs
is the need to
understand and
be understood."

—RALPH NICHOLS

Try something new.

Every now and then, try an unfamiliar activity or hobby. Eat something you've never eaten before. Learn about something online, find a friend who's good at it, and get them to show you the ropes. Stepping out of your comfort zone will teach you how to deal with new and unknown experiences. It will help you be receptive to instruction and guidance. Charismatic people are good at experimenting and trying new things. The farther removed you get from your "typical self," the more you will impress others with your daring nature.

SOCIABLE ⎯⎯⎯⎯→ POPULAR

PERSONAL | SOCIAL | BUSINESS

Don't
assume
everyone
loves pets
or kids
(especially not their own).

Remain cool and in control.

One of the most attractive characteristics of charismatic people is their unfailing ability to stay in control—not of other people, but of themselves. Regardless of hardship or the inconvenience of a situation, keeping your composure is a sign of emotional maturity and sophistication. Conversely, being psychologically volatile, resorting to emotional outbursts and hysteria, is fundamentally unattractive. It communicates to others that you are a person who is erratic and undependable—exactly the opposite of a charismatic person. Remaining cool takes practice. But the payoff in internal serenity and external poise is well worth it.

Always err on the side of kindness.

Let others talk first, then have the final say.

At social engagements—be it a dinner party, a group of people having a drink, a work lunch, or a reception—there will be a lot of people who want to express themselves. Don't contribute to the cacophony; no one will remember what you said (not even you, probably), and there will be fewer chances of someone actually engaging with you. Instead, wait until the racket quiets down, find a sweet spot of momentary silence, and then drop your phrase, idea, or comment. This will make what you say stand out (hopefully, it's something interesting!). Others will have time to process and respond, and you will come across as someone worthy of attention, rather than part of a chorus of disjointed sentences and idle cackling.

SOCIABLE ⎯⎯⎯→ POPULAR

If you need your conversation partner to shut up, don't say it in so many words. Instead, use this cheat sheet.

ANNOYANCE LEVEL	REACTION
Not even caring	"Excuse me, I will be back in a second"
Somewhat annoyed	"Excuse me, I will be back in a second"
Simmering	"Excuse me, I will be back in a second"
Boiling	"Excuse me, I will be back in a second"
Frothing with frustration	"Excuse me, I will be back in a second"

SOCIABLE ⟶ POPULAR

Don't brag.

PERSONAL

SOCIAL

BUSINESS

Own your opinions. Don't say, "I may be wrong" all the time.

Some people make a habit of distancing themselves from whatever they are about to say by issuing an array of disclaimers. These usually begin with, "It's only my opinion," or, "I may be wrong," or, "I don't know much about this, but...." This way, they cannot be held liable for their views. They create exit strategies out of anything they say. Listen to an ambassador talk, or watch a UN conference (both of which epitomize the art of diplomacy and discretion). Notice that no one prefaces their opinion with a disclaimer. To be careful, to avoid offending, or to keep away from confrontation doesn't mean disowning everything important you have to say. You'll just come across as spineless. Say what you truly believe and stand behind it. Otherwise, what's the point of talking?

Be mature— behave like an adult.

PERSONAL

SOCIAL

BUSINESS

Don't linger; make sure you exit at an appropriate time.

Give praise, immediately.

Timing is everything. To praise someone in the moment gives them a jolt of euphoria. Even if they later doubt your sincerity, the feeling your praise gave has stayed with them. That's what matters, much more than the actual or perceived "truth." Don't shy away from giving praise, and doing it on the spot. People will love the momentary elation and want to be around someone who makes them feel that way.

SOCIABLE ⎯⎯⎯⎯→ POPULAR

Offer to help the host.

"I have yet to find the man, however exalted his station, who did not do better work and put forth greater effort under a spirit of approval than under a spirit of criticism."

—CHARLES SCHWAB

Appreciate the other person's time.

When calling a person, ask if it's a good time to talk, especially if you anticipate a long discussion. If you meet them at a party or social gathering, check if they are in the mood for serious conversation by asking if they've got a minute to chat. Just because you're in the mood, don't assume the other person wants to indulge you. They may, but checking shows that you appreciate their time, that you are considerate of their mood, and that you are aware of social conventions.

"It's a done deal, then—you promise never
to put me on hold, and I promise never
to put you on hold."

Prefer positive to negative gossip.

Gossiping is not the most praiseworthy of activities. Most people consider it sly, low-minded, and improper. Even so, very few dislike hearing or telling a good story about someone. Gaining the reputation of being a gossip is unsavory, and you should avoid it at all costs. If, however, you find yourself stuck in a situation where gossip is the topic of the day, try to stick with the positive. Whispering behind someone's back about their achievements or a recent accomplishment can make you look really good—as long as it's done with genuine admiration, not spite and envy.

SOCIABLE ⟶ POPULAR

Don't tell one person how much you dislike another.

PERSONAL | SOCIAL | BUSINESS

"A creative man is motivated by the desire to achieve, not the desire to beat others."

—AYN RAND

Avoid teaming up.

A debate can be an exciting intellectual exercise. Even if it becomes a heated argument, it can still be mentally and emotionally stimulating. This, however, presupposes that all parties involved are of relatively equal stature and can argue in a constructive manner that advances the discussion, rather than their own egos. To aggressively go after a person with the sole intent of demeaning and embarrassing them is a terrible tactic and shows absolutely no social skills. To do so as part of a group is even worse. Teaming up with others and turning them against a single person is an outrageous act of bad manners. Make it a rule never to team up against a single person. Likewise, take the weaker person's side whenever they are being attacked.

PERSONAL

SOCIAL

BUSINESS

Admit your mistakes.

Create intimacy.

One of the oldest tricks for creating a sense of intimacy is to use the word "we" shortly after you've met a person—especially in the presence of someone else. After sharing a brief conversation or activity, refer to it as something that "we" shared. Referring to someone next to you as one half of a "we" triggers in their subconscious a sense of connection and togetherness—even if it's entirely your construct. Be careful, however, not to take liberties. Creating an impression of false or unearned intimacy can be perceived as intrusive and clingy. Avoid coming across as presumptuous.

131

"Hi, I'm Harry Nagle of Zenith Printing and Engraving,
a wholly-owned subsidiary of Krantek Graphics, a
Division of Simpco-Spectrum Incorporated,
part of the Dataphrax Group.
Who are you?"

Always remember to introduce yourself and others in your group.

PERSONAL

SOCIAL

BUSINESS

Be aware of your surroundings.

Being a great communicator isn't just about your message. A lot hinges on the delivery—for instance, good timing. When the person you're speaking to is distracted, the effect of your message can be reduced dramatically. One way to make sure that the time is right is to remain aware of your surroundings. If you see a waiter coming your way, pause before you are interrupted. If you hear your conversation partner's phone ring, ask if they'd like to take the call. You are not just being caring and observant; you are making sure your message is delivered and can have maximum impact.

Don't have a private quarrel in public.

PERSONAL | SOCIAL | BUSINESS

Conditions for giving
your business card:

You have one.

It's factual.

You are important enough.

You've been asked for it, or offered one.

You intend to conduct business.

You are over 30.

It's rectangular and printed on paper.

You didn't make it at an airport booth.

You are not a drug dealer.

You intend to respond.

SOCIABLE $\longrightarrow$ POPULAR

Have someone you trust point out your flaws.

Few things are as refreshing (and useful) as hearing someone tell you the truth about yourself. We constantly invent stories, make excuses, and buy into all sorts of delusions just to live with the one person we can't avoid: ourselves. Having someone else hold up a mirror can be an intimate, and potentially hurtful, exercise, but it will keep your ego in check. Choose someone you absolutely trust, a very close friend or a relative who knows you well.

PERSONAL

137

SOCIABLE $\longrightarrow$ POPULAR

PERSONAL

SOCIAL

BUSINESS

Be ready to accept that you might be wrong.

"You agree with me a lot, Wilkins—I like that in a junior partner."

Don't just apologize;
offer to help.

A sincere apology is a great gesture. Even better is a sincere apology followed by a tangible offer to help. People always trust actions more than words; offering to help make a wrong right will always be appreciated.

Exude trustworthiness and dependability.

PERSONAL

SOCIAL

BUSINESS

Learn some quotes that can spark a conversation.

Quotes are a brilliant way to spark a conversation. They can be funny, pithy, sarcastic, compassionate, or obvious. But most good quotes have one thing in common: They sum up a lot in a few words. Quotes can be used to diffuse an uncomfortable situation, spark a discussion, lend a helping hand of authority, or make you look well-read. They are brilliant because they are short and easy to remember. Choose wisely, and don't worry too much about who said it. Just remember the quote.

SOCIABLE ⟶ POPULAR

As a host, always introduce your guests to one another.

PERSONAL

SOCIAL

BUSINESS

The most important thing:

At a dinner party	Manners
At work	Conscientiousness
With friends	Honesty
In your relationship	Trust
At a social gathering	Attentiveness
At a gallery opening	Mingling
On an airplane	Silence
In a cat café	What?

SOCIABLE ⟶ POPULAR

Leave compliments
with third parties.

If you want to make someone feel good, give them a direct compliment. If you want it to seem especially sincere, compliment the person through a third party, someone you know will pass it on. Any doubt about your intentions will be dispelled. Complimenting someone via a third party also makes you look good in the eyes of that person. They hope you might feel the same way about them. Overall, third-party complimenting is a much more effective way of flattering someone.

Don't ask questions and expect others to answer them without reciprocating the favor.

PERSONAL | SOCIAL | BUSINESS

Don't underestimate others' intelligence.

Becoming an inspirational and charismatic person will boost your confidence. However, if you get so wound up in your reinvented self that your ego inflates beyond repair, you may pay dearly. Regardless of how success-ful you become—how well you end up commanding the social scene—remain constantly aware that the peo-ple around you (even if less gifted and charming) can be equally smart, informed, and contentious. Remain respectful of their intelligence and don't underestimate them, take them for granted, or treat them as anything less than equals.

SOCIABLE ⎯⎯⎯⎯→ POPULAR

Don't be paranoid about a little mess.

Politeness takes time to pay off.

Being pleasant, cordial, and courteous isn't necessarily rewarded on the spot. Some might consider it simply good manners. Others will take your gracious demeanor for granted. Some will not even notice. A few people might find it fake or think you have an ulterior motive. But being consistently polite and tactful will, over time, dispel any suspicions about your intentions. Knowing that you aren't hoping to gain anything from being polite, others will gradually relax and open up to you.

SOCIABLE ⟶ POPULAR

PERSONAL

SOCIAL

BUSINESS

Be patient.

Don't
name-drop.

PERSONAL | SOCIAL | BUSINESS

Pay attention to details.

"Seventy percent
of success in life
is showing up."

—WOODY ALLEN

PERSONAL

SOCIAL

BUSINESS

Praise the host in conversations.

"Continuous effort—not strength or intelligence— is the key to unlocking our potential."

—WINSTON CHURCHILL

PERSONAL

SOCIAL

BUSINESS

From Popular to Socialite

PART THREE

Now that you have left the safety of solitude and graduated from the comfort of intimacy into the unchartered waters of an active, colorful, and diverse social life, it is time to expand your skills and stand the test of being a true socialite. That means no less than being the perfect host, the ideal guest, an engaging conversationalist, and an avid and refined dinner table companion. This section is dedicated to those most elegant and sophisticated traits that a person with a prolific social calendar has to possess. Here's to the afterparties at the Oscars.

PERSONAL

SOCIAL

BUSINESS

"The key with any gift is in the way that you use it. It doesn't define you as a person. Rather, it's an asset to be used judiciously and with an understanding of how it is just a small part of who you are."

— DALE ARCHER

Treat others as ends in themselves, not as means to your ends.

This should go without saying. People are precious beings, whether we like them or not. They deserve better than being reduced to a means of facilitating your goals. You will certainly alienate someone by signaling that their only value lies in "what they bring to the table"—in other words, how they are useful to you. Steer far away from this mindset and focus on making everyone feel special—even if there is no direct benefit to you.

POPULAR ⟶ SOCIALITE

Don't
compare
yourself
to others.

Help someone out when you see them struggling.

When a person is telling a story and you see them getting stuck—looking for the right word, trying to remember the name of a place, or struggling to get their facts straight—come to their rescue if you can. Your help will be appreciated and possibly reciprocated. You will also come across as a great conversationalist and a pleasant, generous person. Letting someone simmer in their awkwardness is unkind; helping makes you the good guy. Lend your assistance gallantly, but don't overshadow them or make them look or feel stupid.

"The test of good manners is to be patient with the bad ones."

—SOLOMON IBN GABIROL

Be humble; all great people are.

PERSONAL

SOCIAL

BUSINESS

Make your compliments about qualities, rather than people.

Complimenting someone is easy—so easy that it can sound forced or insincere. Worse, it can be seen as an attempt to boost your own image. The way around that is to compliment traits or accomplishments, rather than people. For example, instead of expressing your admiration for someone's generosity, mention how highly you esteem generous people. An added advantage: Everyone in the room who considers themselves generous will take it as a personal endorsement. Be sure to do this artfully and sparingly to avoid being obvious.

Care about every person, not just the one you're interested in.

PERSONAL

SOCIAL

BUSINESS

Be authoritative, but considerate.

Charisma is all about achieving balance—between bold-ness and compassion, authority and thoughtfulness. Being confident can distort your ability to be atten-tive and patient. Too much authoritativeness and your demands or expectations can come across as unreason-able. On the other hand, worrying too much about others' opinions can derail you. The trick is to balance your idea, plan, or intention with consideration for other people. Remain assertive, but don't offend others or overstretch their abilities.

Don't micromanage others.

PERSONAL

SOCIAL

BUSINESS

"It's agreed, then. I'll have my lawyer wish
your lawyer a happy birthday."

Be generous with your time, resources, and attention.

Generosity is universally thought of as admirable. But many people think generosity is limited to the basic act of giving, or giving away. Generosity is much more than that. It is a state of mind. People who are generous in one area of their life (say, financially) tend to be generous in other areas (empathy, support). Generosity is an extremely attractive quality. In the short term, it makes others feel good about what they are receiving. In the long term (and this is what matters most), generosity shows you are a confident and bold person, one who doesn't cling to what they have for fear of losing it, who has limitless emotional resources, who knows that they can easily regain what they give away.

POPULAR ⎯⎯⎯→ SOCIALITE

Don't be self-important.

Match your conversation partner's mood and mindset.

Humans are social animals, and social animals imitate one another. By mirroring someone's mood, you are making them feel endorsed. You are reinforcing their state of mind, giving the impression that you understand and support them. You communicate that you stand united with them, whatever mood they're in—and that is enormously comforting. In conversations, try to match your partner's or group's general disposition. If they are feeling downcast, treating them with contempt or lightheartedness is not only inconsiderate and counterproductive, it is rude. It can make the general mood even more unpleasant. If, on the other hand, they are feeling upbeat and cheerful, bringing them down will seem annoying, even hostile.

POPULAR ⟶ SOCIALITE

Handle being the center of attention with grace.

"Charm is a way of getting the answer 'yes' without asking a clear question."

—ALBERT CAMUS

Show empathy, but temper
it with a bit of cynicism.

Empathy is the fundamental quality that makes us compassionate. The ability to relate to another person and their state of mind is central in human interaction. Lack of empathy is the first step to being a sociopath. But being empathetic doesn't mean being an empty container for everyone else's emotions. Too much empathy—especially when the situation is far removed from your own experience—can come across as fake. You have to know where to draw the line. Adding just a dash of cynicism will help you and your conversation partner see the larger picture (the world doesn't begin and end with them). It will reveal a positive or funny side to an otherwise dramatic story, and even alleviate some of the gravity weighing them down. Finally, remember that people are surrounded by feigned emotion (from sales clerks to politicians). They are invariably drawn to people who seem (and are) real.

Charismatic Person vs. Sociopath

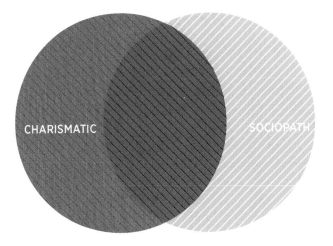

CHARISMATIC

SOCIOPATH

POPULAR $\longrightarrow$ SOCIALITE

"That was just Fred having his little joke."

Don't tell the same stories to the same crowd.

Repetition breeds tedium. Telling the same stories to the same people time and again will turn those stories into a joke. Strive to renew your material. If you find it hard to conjure up new stories, an old trick is to change the perspective on the existing ones. Add some information or details that were missing before. If all else fails, there's nothing wrong with weaving some fictional element into a true story. Writers and artists all pump up the drama, even when dealing with facts. Since you're not testifying in court, there's nothing morally wrong with "enriching" your stories with a bit of tall tale.

Be smart about assigning seats at the dinner table.

Learn to read others by their appearance.

How we dress is a form of nonverbal communication. People make statements by the way they curate their appearance, with the most informal and careless-looking choice of attire tells a story. Even a look that says "I don't care about how I look" is a representation of what that person believes. Learning to read these subtle statements gives you a lot of information about the other person, and will arm you with a wealth of conversation topics. Next time you are with a large group of people, see if you can make up a story in your head about each person's choice of attire. You'll soon realize that picking something to wear is not as simple as you thought.

PERSONAL

SOCIAL

BUSINESS

Exchange contact details discreetly.

Don't question others' sincerity.

Few things can be as alienating as questioning another person's intentions. Doubting someone may be productive if they're genuinely wrong, but personally attacking their credibility, especially in public, can have disastrous consequences. Nobody likes being discredited—less so in the company of others. And after all, you can't read someone else's mind. Only they know for sure what their intentions are. If you have suspicions about someone's sincerity, keep them to yourself and act accordingly.

PERSONAL

SOCIAL

BUSINESS

"Know your enemy and know yourself and in 100 battles you will never be in peril."

—SUN TZU

Don't be
a bully.

PERSONAL

SOCIAL

BUSINESS

Don't shy away from a
sincere apology.

To apologize—sincerely and in a timely manner—
shows others that you are generous, open-minded, and
kindhearted—the traits all charismatic people share.
Negotiating your accountability, making excuses, and
denying your culpability sends the message that what is
clearly important to others is insignificant to you. That
makes others feel *they* are insignificant to you, and is
certain to alienate them. If you are unsure about your culpability, or believe that being blamed will not serve the
truth, communicate that fact soberly, in a spirit of cooper-
ation and mutual desire to uncover the facts. At the very
least, you can say, "I'm sorry you feel that way," without
actually shouldering the blame. But remember that, as a
general rule, taking the blame for something that wasn't
your fault will make you look better in others' eyes.

Choose your words wisely.

PERSONAL

SOCIAL

BUSINESS

Be optimistic.

We all know people who make us feel gloomy and others who make us feel light. Much like laughing and yawning, optimism is contagious. Being hopeful, confident, and upbeat transfers to others around you. When people are in the company of a cheerful, bright, and confident individual, they instinctively share in that optimism, even if they're not exactly sure why. If you are the cause of their optimism, good feelings will be associated with you. In the future, thoughts of you will conjure feelings of lightness and well-being. Try to be optimistic and inspire people around you to be the same—you will always be in good company.

Don't whine.

Create a shared history.

A brilliant way of getting closer to someone is to create the illusion of a shared history. Shared experiences
inspire trust, even if the experiences are few and took
place a long time ago. Some people refer to their relationships with others with phrases like, "We go wa-a-ay
back." Even people who met a long time ago, and have
scarcely kept in touch with each other, still value their
shared history. If you've only met someone recently, you
can create a shared history by finding a common experience or memory. Perhaps you both follow the same sports
team and recall the last time they won a championship.
Maybe you both loved a vacation in Spain or enjoy the
books of a particular author. Thinking you both hold the
same things dear can inspire intimacy.

"*Tonight's small-talk topics are condominiums in Florida and tax-free municipals. Have fun.*"

PERSONAL

SOCIAL

BUSINESS

"There is only one thing in life worse than being talked about, and that is not being talked about."

—OSCAR WILDE

Weave some storytelling into your answers.

A list of standard questions asked at social engagements would not be longer than half a page. "Where are you from?" "What do you do for a living?" "Do you like your job?" "Where do you live?" These are the openers everyone uses. Answering these questions with single-word responses automatically signals that you are tired of the same old questions. While this may be the case, there's nothing more off-putting than indirectly telling another person they are trite and boring. To prevent that, enrich your answers with some storytelling. "I work in a department store, and just the other day someone came in and ..." Storytelling will delight the other person, highlight your ability to turn something mundane into an interesting episode, and unfailingly trigger a genuinely interesting exchange.

Know when a conversation has come to an end.

Command respect.

We are drawn to people whose overall attitude communicates respect. Respect, of course, must be earned. A good start is to practice mindful self-respect. Feel confident in your abilities and you will act the right way. You will be compassionate with others, serious when the situation demands it, courteous in all situations, bold when necessary. As people observe your everyday exemplary behavior, they will start to respect you.

Don't feed your ego.

Flatter, but do it sincerely and with authority.

Flattery that comes off as absolutely sincere is a hard thing to master. Complimenting, congratulating, and praising have become so ubiquitous that people know when they are simply being wooed. To let people know they are sincerely being commended, develop a two-tier plan: For the first tier, be courteous by applauding every-day things, such as someone's appearance. Even if the praise is perceived as unnecessary, it will still make the person feel good. Our brains are wired that way. Do it with grace and only when you mean it. For the second tier, flat-ter someone for more significant accomplishments, such as a job promotion. But do so with the self-assured tone of a person who can afford to extend their respect to others.

195

Don't come across like a salesman.

Find the Cretin.
A multiple-choice question.

You have just finished having dinner at a nice restaurant and are walking out. It's a rainy and cold night. Neither you nor your date has a car. You both live far away. What do you do?

a. *You open your wallet and take out two $5 bills. You fold them and put them in your date's palm, whispering meaningfully, "For your cab." You take off.*

b. *You two-finger whistle and swiftly hail a cab that's passing by. You rush inside the cab, lower the window, and wave good-bye.*

c. *You ask the restaurant if they have an umbrella you can borrow, go outside, and find a cab. You open the door for your date, ask your date's address and give it to the driver. You then close the door and take down the cab's number plate.*

d. *You hail a cab, rush yourself and your date inside, and give the driver your home address.*

POPULAR ⟶ SOCIALITE

*"No trouble at all, Boss.
Call me anytime."*

Work hard— and don't make a big deal of it.

PERSONAL

SOCIAL

BUSINESS

Make sure you elaborate on your compliments.

Praising someone's professional accomplishment, personal milestone, or even choice of garment is an extremely effective way to boost their self-confidence. As a result, it makes them positively disposed toward you—more open, more interested, and more congenial. But if a one-liner can work well, following up your initial remark with a qualifying statement about what you find praiseworthy, and what inspired you to make your statement in the first place, will be truly impressive. It can be as simple as, "I love that hat. It makes you look like a movie star."

Come across as a generous leader.

Find a lesson in failure.

Charismatic people are constantly engaged in bold pursuits that may or may not succeed. That daring attitude is a trait other people find attractive. Nobody likes to fail, and yet, it is through failure that we learn life's lessons. From emotional separations to professional disappointments, the things we get wrong inform our future decisions and gradually build our wisdom. So keep a positive attitude about failure. Don't fear it, don't deny it, acknowledge its usefulness. If you embrace the knowledge that some of your projects will fail, when the moment comes, you will be prepared to make the most of failure. You can accept it, learn from it, and then leave it behind.

Don't
overreact.

PERSONAL | SOCIAL | BUSINESS

Be absolutely honest.

In an age of perpetual trickery, nothing is as refreshing as a hearty serving of truth. Honesty is sometimes
uncomfortable, even painful. But when choosing between
being a cowardly minion and being a person of substance,
you would be well advised to select the latter. The path
to becoming substantial—and bold—lies in being utterly
honest when the situation calls for it. Remember, though,
that being honest does not mean deliberately caus-
ing pain. Compassion should always be the companion
of honesty.

"There is a kind of beauty in imperfection."

—CONRAD HALL

PERSONAL

SOCIAL

BUSINESS

Don't exert pressure.

Grant autonomy.

People have fought wars to attain and maintain freedom. But freedom doesn't only happen on the grand social scale; it also exists in everyday things, such as the ability to choose one's working hours, or to go out for a few hours without feeling answerable to an overbearing partner. Charismatic people never try to suffocate others by limiting their freedom, sanctioning their independence, or punishing autonomy. People were not made to live in captivity. The more freedom you give other people, the more you're allowing them to be themselves and flourish. Granting autonomy makes others happy, and makes you look kind, benevolent, and trusting.

Don't doubt yourself in public.

Be fun.

Being fun is not the same as being a lightweight, a clown, or a fool. Being fun is a vibe you exude that makes people around you relax, be themselves, open up. Be fun but courteous, kind, and polite; know when to draw the line. Being fun can be easily combined with seriousness. Some of the most charismatic people are extremely serious about their goals, but that doesn't make them boring and somber. Quite the contrary. Fun people can be effective, interesting, smart, and resolute while still being pleasant, enjoyable, and positive.

209

Act like you own the room, but don't overstep.

"Congratulations! You ran through pride, lust,
envy, gluttony, wrath, avarice, and sloth . . .
all in one evening!"

"There can be no power without mystery. There must always be a 'something' which others cannot altogether fathom, which puzzles them, stirs them, and rivets their attention...."

—CHARLES DE GAULLE

Lead by example.

Famed statesmen do it; legendary military leaders do it; charismatic entrepreneurs do it. Such people never expect others to do what they can't or won't do themselves. They master and demonstrate the attributes they expect to find in others—whether it's a quality, like honesty, or a particular job skill. Learning a new skill (or even trying to) shows that you don't set double standards, don't make unreasonable demands, and don't hesitate to get your hands dirty.

POPULAR ⟶ SOCIALITE

Give more than you receive.

"Be a yardstick of quality. Some people aren't used to an environment where excellence is expected."

—STEVE JOBS

PERSONAL

SOCIAL

BUSINESS

Learn the customs.

Every place, every group, every business has its own moral and behavioral codes. Disrespecting them, even out of ignorance, will only brand you as ignorant. Before venturing into the unknown—whether it's a new professional environment, a foreign land, or meeting friends that observe a code of conduct different from yours—do a bit of research. Find out how *they* do things. If it's not possible or agreeable to do as they do, you'll at least be prepared to excuse yourself, preemptively explaining your differences, and thus showing respect for others. Even as a host, make sure to acknowledge your guests' differences. It is a little trick of great manners: When in Rome, do as the Romans.

POPULAR ⟶ SOCIALITE

Are you traveling?
Don't make a fool of yourself.

In Mexico they'll think you a snob if
you ask for a fork and knife.

In Bulgaria it's considered rude to bring
yellow flowers to your host.

In Tanzania it's improper to show the soles
of your feet when dining on the floor.

In Japan, never show up late.

Be witty.

Act "as if."

If you don't feel confident, bold, and charismatic in a particular situation, imagine a leader you admire, maybe even a character from a book or movie. What would they do in this situation? How would they act? Play the scene out in your head, and then act like that character. Act as if you are confident. Act as if you know exactly what to do. Act as if you are the most charismatic person in the room. It doesn't mater if you feel like you're faking it; most people have that feeling much of the time. Our actions are based largely on habit, and you can change your habits. Act as if you are the person you want to be, and you will become that person.

"Life is 10 percent of
what happens to me
and 90 percent of
how I react to it."

—JOHN MAXWELL

Don't advertise your intelligence.

PERSONAL

SOCIAL

BUSINESS

True charisma is invisible.

Charisma should not be displayed like a badge of honor. It operates under the radar; it is not to meant be advertised. There's a saying: "Money talks. But big money whispers." When you feel confident in your own skin—with who you are, with how you are—there is no need to turn up the volume and let everyone in the room know. Your qualities will shine through. Being charismatic is nothing to brag about; it is the self-assurance that there is no need to brag. Charisma shines through in subtle nuances, in small gestures, in common courtesy. There is nothing pompous about charisma.

Don't be presumptuous.

PERSONAL

SOCIAL

BUSINESS

The ideal handshake

POPULAR ⟶ SOCIALITE

Be a bit mysterious.

The unknown is inherently more compelling than the known. Injecting a small dose of mystery into any story lends excitement, arouses curiosity, and creates an irresistible aura. We ourselves are stories; we are the accumulation of experiences, fables, incidents, anecdotes, and memories. Keeping certain parts of ourselves hidden is not only normal and necessary; it's a genuine way to inspire interest and even fascination. Curiosity is a strong motivator. It pays to keep people guessing about you.

Be vigilant and adaptive.

Reward effort, not just results.

When someone is making an effort, they are spending time and skill. No matter if the task is as everyday as setting the table, or as complicated as launching a business project. Whatever the magnitude of the task, it's important to recognize effort. Don't wait until the full results are in before you give credit. This will keep everyone motivated. People will be happier and more fulfilled. The final results will be better for everyone.

Charisma Attained.

PART FOUR

There is just one last thing that you need to remember. After you've learned all the etiquette rules; tried, failed and eventually succeeded in an array of social settings and circles; mastered the art of combining conviviality with enigmatic magnetism; and learned how to finally relax and exude that air of effortlessness – it's time make a mental note. Wherever you are, with as many or as few people, intimately or in a room full of strangers: to be memorable, to leave a lasting impression and to be thought of as a charismatic and charming person you need to do one more thing...

BE
BO

LD.

CPSIA information can be obtained at www.ICGtesting.com
Printed in the USA
BVOW11s2346051115

425548BV00002B/2/P

9 781623 156350